A beginner's guide Sushi

Written by James Goodman

Food produced at Colchester Institute, Centre for Hospitality and Food Studies, UK –
a government designated centre of vocational excellence, by Malcolm Long, Senior Lecturer

KUDOS

Kudos is an imprint of Top That! Publishing plc.
Tide Mill Way, Woodbridge, Suffolk, IP12 IAP, UK
www.kudosbooks.com

contents

introduction

For the millions who love it, eating sushi can be a near spiritual experience. The ingredients are the very best, and it is important that they are respectfully handled.

The glistening, perfect pieces of food are arranged on serving plates with studied attention to detail and philosophical meaning. Sushi chefs may train for years before they are allowed to handle a sushi knife.

However, you don't have to get all that serious at home. To enjoy sushi as high art, treat yourself to a restaurant meal with an expert chef. For your own enjoyment, make it yourself at home. Basic sushi techniques are remarkably easy and enjoyable and the results are delicious.

Often, when people hear 'sushi', they think 'raw fish,' but a Japanese-style preparation of raw fish is properly called 'sashimi'. Sushi often contains uncooked fish, but several of the most popular preparations are vegetarian. It is actually the vinegar-infused rice, combined with premium-quality raw or cooked fish and vegetables, which is central to all sushi dishes.

Sushi is something that everyone can enjoy and the aim here is to introduce you to it. Use this book as a guide which will take you through the basics of shopping and the all-important preparation of the ingredients, enabling you to make the most popular sushi forms.

beginnings

Sushi began as a method of preserving fish and there is evidence to suggest that this began as early as the second century in China.

The ancient process involved using cleaned, raw fish which were then pressed between layers of salt and weighted with a stone. After a few weeks, the stone was removed and replaced with a light cover, and a few months after that, the fermented fish was considered ready to eat.

Initially rice was used merely as a means to begin the fermentation process and was discarded later. Eventually, this was seen as unnecessarily wasteful so the rice was eaten as well. It is believed that sushi was introduced into Japan in about the seventh century AD, although the exact date is not clear.

A nineteenth-century chef by the name of Yohei is credited with serving sushi in its present form and foregoing the fermentation process in favour of preparing the rice in vinegar. This new method of serving sushi fish became extremely popular and two distinct styles emerged. The Kansai style, named after the Kansai region where Osaka is located, uses wooden boxes to press the rice and fish together.

This type of sushi is called Hako-Zushi. Historically, this style owes much to the rice merchants who traded in Osaka. With more rice available to the populace, it is no surprise that this type of sushi consisted primarily of seasoned rice mixed with other ingredients to form decorative, delicious packages.

The other predominant style of sushi, Edo, originated in Tokyo (which was formerly known as Edo). Its situation next to a bay, rich with fish and shellfish, led to the development of sushi. With a select piece of seafood placed on only a small pad of seasoned rice, Nigiri sushi is one example which is now popular in sushi bars around the world.

Fast food sushi bars and restaurants are by no means a new invention. Sushi stalls were emerging almost everywhere in Edo by the middle of the nineteenth century. With handy wheels on the stalls, the sushi traders could move around to the most profitable spots. Without tables or chairs there was little formality. Customers used their fingers to dip sushi in the communal soy sauce, a tradition that certainly wouldn't stand up to today's hygiene standards.

After the Kanto earthquake in 1923, actual sushi bars spread in popularity. Equipped with chairs and tables, they allowed customers to choose to sit to eat, although many continued to consume their food outside.

By the 1960s people turned against the informality of eating while standing, and seated restaurants became the acceptable way to eat sushi. Today, there is a vast array of establishments that sell sushi – restaurants, stalls and even grocery stores have all helped to make the food readily available for everyone to enjoy.

health benefits

Not only does sushi taste great, it is also healthy and nutritious. Health-conscious individuals find that sushi allows them to have a nutritious meal without consuming excessive amounts of fat, cholesterol, sodium, or calories.

Sushi embraces simple, healthy ingredients such as seafood, seaweed, rice, and vegetables, carefully seasoned and arranged to satisfy all the senses. Sushi is a great choice, not just for calorie counters, but also for those following more specific nutritional guidelines.

Even the fattiest varieties of fish used in sushi – tuna, salmon, and eel – contain fewer than 200 calories per 1 g serving, packing in the nutritional power of protein, B-vitamins and minerals, and Omega-3 fatty acids, and playing an enormous role in maintaining a healthy heart and metabolism in general. Nori, rice and vegetables add only a further 150 calories per serving. These calories provide more vitamins, minerals and fibre, and provide a good source of carbohydrates to complement the fish protein. Even wasabi can claim its own small health benefit, being rich in vitamin C.

food safety

Many sushi dishes are made using raw fish, which is a high-risk food product. There is nothing frightening about handling or eating high-risk food products, as long as you purchase, prepare and store them correctly.

Food-borne illness is caused by contaminated food and often affects the stomach or intestines. When your body detects that you have eaten something harmful it tries to get rid of the food using the quickest method.

There are two types of illnesses linked to food poisoning and food-borne disease. Food poisoning is caused by eating food contaminated by harmful substances or by harmful bacteria that are living on the food, while a food-borne disease is caused by consuming food or water that is carrying harmful micro-organisms.

Bacteria are invisible life forms that live on, and in, our bodies and throughout the natural world.

There are thousands of different types of bacteria, many serving useful purposes. A very small proportion is, however, harmful and causes food-borne illness or causes food to perish.

Bacteria can multiply rapidly by dividing into two. As each bacterium needs only ten to twenty minutes to multiply, it is possible for one bacterium to lead to the production of millions of bacteria within a few hours.

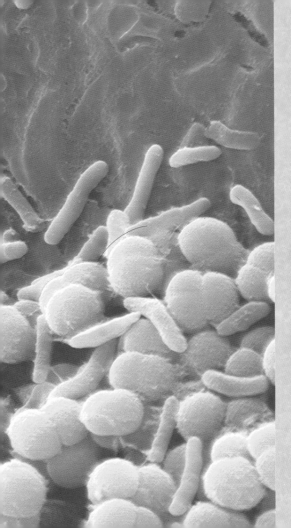

bacterial food poisoning

Bacterial food poisoning occurs under the following conditions:

- If food is eaten after it has been contaminated by pathogenic bacteria.
- If food is stored in conditions that allow the bacteria to multiply to levels that cause illness.
- If harmful bacteria are not destroyed, for example, by adequate cooking.

Food poisoning bacteria multiply when they have ideal conditions. These are:

- Food
- Moisture
- Warmth
- Time

When food poisoning bacteria spend enough time on the right types of food at ambient temperatures, they can quickly multiply to dangerous levels.

preventing food poisoning

Purchase produce from a good supplier, or supermarket. Be confident about their food hygiene standards. Should you have concerns, let them know what you are using it for. If the produce is unsuitable they should be able to tell you.

Take food home immediately after shopping and refrigerate, or freeze foods that need it right away. Wash all fruit and vegetables before eating or cooking them.

Remember, dirt carries germs so keep working areas clean.

Thoroughly clean surfaces which come into contact with cooked food, for example chopping boards and knives. The use of clean, sterilised equipment prevents germs spreading to other food, where they could multiply. Never use the same chopping board, or knife, when preparing raw and cooked food. Never use equipment which has been used for raw food, for cooked food unless it has been thoroughly cleaned.

storing food

Germs are very good at growing in warm temperatures. This means that you must store food below 7°C, in the refrigerator where germs cannot grow.

Never leave cooked, or raw, food out – always put food in the refrigerator as quickly as possible. There are a lot of germs on raw food so always keep cooked food covered and away from raw food. Wash your hands before touching different foods.

sushi etiquette

Traditionally, sushi is eaten with the fingers. When ordered, it usually comes in pairs – these symbolise husband and wife – a Japanese wife would make two of each item in anticipation of her husband returning for dinner.

- Sushi is accompanied by soy sauce, wasabi and pickled ginger. The wasabi is mixed with the soy sauce in a small bowl. The sushi, however, is not to be dunked in the soy sauce, as this will cause the rice to crumble. Nigiri sushi with fish on top is turned upside down before dipping, so that the soy sauce will season the fish only. The ginger is then eaten between mouthfuls to cleanse the palate and aid digestion.

- Chopsticks should be used when taking food from a shared or communal plate. Use the reverse end of the chopsticks rather than the ends that go into your mouth. The sushi should then be eaten with the fingers.

- Never bite into the food and then replace it on your plate. Once you have picked something up, you should eat it all.

- Also be careful never to leave rice at the end of a meal. Leaving any kind of food is considered rude – rice especially so.

- Finally, do not ask for a knife. This would imply that the food is so tough it cannot be properly eaten without one.

basic utensils

One of the advantages of making sushi is the small amount of equipment required.

The utensils needed to make sushi are probably already in your kitchen drawers and cupboards. Substitutes for those that are not handy can be easily found.

When making substitutes, however, avoid metal utensils whenever possible. Vinegar is a major ingredient in all sushi dishes and, if you prepare sushi with metal utensils, the taste of the finished product will be adversely affected.

chopping board (manaita)

Owning a manaita, or chopping board, (preferably about 25 cm x 40 cm) is an absolute must. It is essential for a variety of tasks as it is used when filleting, de-boning, and slicing fish; as a cutting surface when preparing vegetables and as a flat surface upon which nearly every type of sushi is made.

fan (uchiwa)

A fan, known as uchiwa, is used to drive off moisture and encourage evaporation to get the right texture and flavour of sushi rice. This fan is made of bamboo ribs covered with either paper or silk, sometimes beautifully patterned. If no uchiwa is available, an electric fan or even a magazine will do.

rice cooker

Owning a rice cooker makes things a whole lot easier, and is worth every penny. A must for the avid sushi maker, as it will save you time and headaches. Alternatively, you could use a pot for cooking the rice but ensure it has a snugly fitting lid with a bottom and walls that will evenly distribute the heat. The size of the pot depends on how much rice you are going to make. Generally speaking, the more you cook the better the chances of ending up with delicious rice. Rice swells as it cooks, increasing anywhere from two to three times its original volume.

rice cooling tub (hangiri)

A hangiri is used for cooling the vinegared rice, giving it perfect texture and gloss. It is made of cypress, and bound with copper hoops, but any wooden or plastic container can be used instead. The more air that can get to the rice the better, so make sure you use a wide container. Thoroughly wipe the inside of the tub with a clean cloth soaked in vinegared water before using. Unless the inside of the tub is moistened, rice will stick to its surface, making mixing difficult.

spatula (shamoji)

A flat, spoon-like spatula called a shamoji is used to fluff, mix and serve the sushi rice. Traditionally the spatula is a symbol of the housewife's position in the household. Shaped like a large, flattened spoon, this utensil is particularly suited to handling rice. As a wooden paddle absorbs flavours easily, it is best to use a new one, or keep one set aside for your rice making. Avoid those that have been used for other types of cooking. You could also use an ordinary spoon but only a wooden or plastic one. Before using a rice paddle to scoop up hot rice or mix sushi rice, be sure to thoroughly moisten it, otherwise the rice will stick to the paddle.

sushi mat
(makisu)

A makisu, used to roll maki sushi, is
the first piece of equipment that you are likely to
work with. There is other equipment which may be
useful to obtain later but this item is essential. Makisu are
generally less than a 30 cm square in size and are made of
thin pieces of bamboo tied together with string.

sushi knife (sashimibouchou)

The only way to cut cleanly, and accurately, is to use steel
knives of good quality, and whetstones, and you should
sharpen your blades yourself. Good Japanese knives are a
development from forging the Japanese sword, which is
famous for its sharpness. The classic sushi knife is called a
sashimibouchou knife, but any sharp knife will do. A
sashimibouchou is made of razor-sharp carbon steel with
a ho wood handle that doesn't get slippery
when wet.

the bare essentials

Whether making vegetarian or fish-based sushi, you'll need the following ingredients to get started.

rice (kome)

The taste and texture of cooked rice is central to the sushi experience. Therefore the selection of the proper type and quality of this all-important ingredient must be made with great care. Because rice is cultivated over a wide area there are innumerable brands and types to choose from. This should not deter you. Simply stated, the best rice to buy is white, short grain, Japanese rice that states 'for sushi'. Its high content of amylopectin, a glutinous starch, helps it stick together. Don't use long-grain, wild, brown, or instant rice – they're just not sticky enough. A well-stocked oriental food shop or top supermarket will be the best source for the finest sushi rice.

rice vinegar (su)

Japanese rice vinegar can be bought seasoned or plain. It's easy to season to taste (we'll tell you how a little later), so go ahead and buy the plain variety. Rice vinegar is, without doubt, the single most important flavouring in sushi. It perfectly complements the taste and texture of cooked rice and the tang of the wasabi. Rice vinegar also has many nutritional benefits, not the least of which is that it aids digestion.

Other vinegars such as wine and apple should not be used as their fragances are too overpowering and obliterate the delicate flavours of sushi.

seaweed sheets (nori)

Sheets of dried laver, called nori, are used for rolling up seasoned rice and a number of other ingredients to make many varieties of sushi. To make sheets of nori, seaweed is gathered from the sea, washed and then chopped into small pieces. After being washed in fresh water to remove any salt, the pieces of seaweed are then placed into a large, square frame and dried. The resulting sheets are cut and packaged.

pickled ginger (gari)

Pickled ginger (gari) has a clean, sweet taste that clears the palate between courses of a sushi meal. The root of the ginger plant (shoga) is familiar to most western cooks. It plays an important part in Japanese cooking, lending a touch of sharpness and aroma to many dishes. This is particularly true of sushi. When eating sushi, pickled ginger slices called sudori shoga (gari) are always served. Taken between bites, it freshens the palate and aids digestion. It can be bought ready-made or you can make your own using the recipe on the next page.

make your own gari
ingredients

- Pickled ginger slices
- 1 fresh ginger root, peeled
- 3 tablespoons rice vinegar
- 2 tablespoons Niban dashi stock (p. 29)
- 1 tablespoon sugar
- 1 teaspoon salt

method

In a bowl, combine the vinegar and stock. Add the sugar and stir until dissolved. Set aside. Peel and slice the ginger root as thin as paper. Soak in cold water for five minutes. Dip the slices in boiling water for 3–5 seconds. While still hot, add the slices to the vinegar and stock marinade. Marinate for at least thirty minutes, the longer, the better. Drain the slices and serve. Pickled ginger slices can be made in any quantity and refrigerated for future use.

soy sauce (shoyu)

Soy sauce (shoyu) is the standard dipping sauce for sushi. The best brands for sushi are made in Japan; many Chinese soy sauces are thick and sweet, and not appropriate for sushi. Soy sauce is the familiar rich, brown sauce made from a fermented mixture of brine, wheat malt and soybeans. While the taste of soy sauce may differ from brand to brand, generally speaking there are two basic types: the dark-coloured koi kuchi shoyu and the light-coloured usu kuchi shoyu. Koi kuchi shoyu serves for almost all home cooking and is used to season many dishes, including sushi. The usu kuchi shoyu is less fragrant and contains more salt, and is not suitable for serving with sushi.

wasabi

Wasabi is green Japanese horseradish. Wasabi has the power to efface the smell of fish. It is an absolute must for making nigiri sushi and mixed with soy sauce makes a delicious sauce for sashimi. Wasabi grows along the banks of pure, cold streams. It grows only around 2 cm a year, taking several years to reach maturity. In Japan it is cultivated in mountain terraces through which mountain water is allowed to run. It is claimed that the sharp taste of wasabi stimulates the stomach, aids digestion, and neutralises any poison.

Fresh wasabi is hard to obtain in the West, but there are substitutes. One type is available in a powder which is mixed with water until it becomes a thick paste. The other type comes ready prepared.

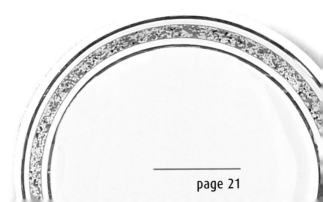

other ingredients

There are many other ingredients which can be used to prepare, and enjoy, sushi. Once again, the best sources are Japanese food shops and supermarkets.

bonito shavings (katsuo-bushi)

The shaved flakes of dried bonito are very aromatic and tasty. They can be eaten sprinkled over hot rice, but most importantly they are used, along with kombo, to make the basic Japanese stocks called 'dashi'.

bean curd (tofu)

In Japan, tofu is one of the staples of the traditional diet. Eaten as it is with a variety of flavourings, or cooked in any number of ways, it is a delicious accompaniment to any Japanese meal. There are two types of tofu used in making sushi, but the most common is a thin slice of deep-fried tofu, seasoned on the sweet side, then used to form a small pouch which is, in turn, filled with sushi rice and other ingredients.

bamboo shoots
(takenoko)

When fresh shoots are not available you can use dried, bottled, or tinned varieties. Preserved shoots often have a white substance clinging to the pieces, or suspended in the canning water. This is not harmful but it does detract from the appearance and taste. To remove this, wash the shoots in fresh water and boil them for twenty minutes. Using our simple recipe on the right, preserved bamboo shoots can be made to taste almost as good as fresh shoots. They should always be cooked and seasoned before eating.

seasoned bamboo shoots
ingredients

- 150 g bamboo shoots, cut into bite-sized pieces
- 1 cup stock
- $\frac{1}{2}$ teaspoon salt
- 2 teaspoons sugar
- 1 teaspoon mirin (sweet rice wine)
- 2 teaspoons shoyu

method

Over a low heat mix the stock, mirin and shoyu in a saucepan, season with salt and sugar. Add the bamboo shoots and cook until the liquid has reduced by half. Remove from the heat and allow to cool before using.

tamago yaki
ingredients
- 4 large eggs
- 1 tablespoon sugar
- 1/2 tablespoon salt
- 4 tablespoons dashi or stock
- 1 teaspoon mirin
- 1/2 teaspoon shoyu

method
Beat the ingredients together until well mixed. Heat some oil in a frying pan. Once hot, add a third of the mixture and swirl to cover the base. When it has set, roll it and push it back to the other side of the pan. Re-oil and pour in more of the mixture making sure it also gets under the roll. Roll again, but to your side of the pan. Do the same until all the mixture is used. Allow to cool and use it either in nigiri sushi or as a side dish with daikon and shoyu sauce.

eggs (tamago)
Eggs are used to make the special Japanese omelette utilised to such great effect in sushi. The slightly sweet flavour and bright, yellow colour of a Japanese omelette serves to balance the taste and appearance of a sushi meal. There are many varieties of sushi and many ways to prepare eggs to complement this rice dish. These recipes are just some ways eggs can be used in sushi.

japanese mushrooms (shiitake)

Although fresh shiitake are delicious, dried ones are used when preparing sushi, because the mushrooms' taste and aroma increases when drying. When selecting dried shiitake, make sure they are thoroughly dried, feature a hood that is brown and slightly glossy, have short stems and a rich aroma. The thicker the hood of the mushroom, the better the taste and aroma!

usayaki tamago
ingredients

· 1 egg
· 1 egg yolk
· 1 teaspoon cornflour
· 1 tablespoon vegetable oil
· 1 tablespoon water

method

Dissolve the cornflour in water. Mix all the other ingredients except the oil and add the cornflour mixture. Heat the oil in a pan and pour in enough egg mixture to coat the pan thinly. As it begins to set, turn it over with a fork. Do not let it get crisp or overdone. Cut the round edges off the omelette to make thin omelette parcels or cut into fine shreds.

seasoned shiitake
ingredients
- 10 pieces dried shiitake
- 4–5 tablespoons sugar
- 4–5 tablespoons shoyu
- 4 teaspoons mirin

method
Rinse the mushrooms with water and soak until they have returned to their natural shape and become soft to the touch (approx thirty minutes). Remove the stems. Place the reconstituted mushroom hoods in a small saucepan and add enough of the soaking water to cover. Bring the water to the boil. Reduce the heat and simmer for twenty minutes. Add the sugar and shoyu. Continue to simmer until the liquid has evaporated, stirring from time to time to stop the mushrooms sticking to the pan. Add the mirin and move the saucepan from side to side so that the boiled-down liquid sticks to the mushrooms. Cool and cut to the desired size.

kelp (kombo)
Kombo, or kelp, thrives only in the coldest seawater. The dark brown leaves are harvested during the summer. After a thorough drying in the sun they are cut, folded, and sealed in airtight packages. The dark, dried leaves are among the basic ingredients of the stocks that are used in Japanese cooking.

leaves (ha)
Cut out leaves are used to separate different types of sushi when they are arranged together. They keep the different tastes from mixing, prevent the sushi from discolouring, and add an accent of colour to the arrangement.

lotus root (renkon)

The crunchy root of the lotus plant can be cooked in a variety of ways – simmered with vegetables, dressed with vinegar or sesame seeds, or deep-fried as tempura. It is also used in rolled sushi and scattered sushi.

mirin

Mirin is a sweet wine made from various types of glutinous rice. It is one of the basic ingredients of the vinegar dressing for sushi rice, adding aroma, a touch of sweetness, and a pearl-like lustre to the finished product. There are two types of Mirin: hon mirin and shin mirin. Their flavours are different, but either can be used for making sushi rice.

natto

The fermented soya bean product called natto has a very distinctive aroma and is quite glutinous. It often makes an appearance in the traditional Japanese breakfast. Like most soya bean products, it is highly nutritious.

sesame seeds (goma)

Sesame seeds add flavour and aroma to many sushi dishes. While it is fine to use sesame seeds as they are, roasting them enhances their characteristics and flavour. To roast, simply heat a small frying pan, toss in the seeds, stir constantly until golden, and then remove from the pan.

ichiban dashi:
stock for clear soup

ingredients

- 750 ml water
- 10 cm square piece of dried kombo
- approximately 15 g katsuo-bushi

method

Bring the water to the boil in a saucepan. Wipe the kombo clean with a damp cloth. Make a few slashes in the leaf with the tip of a knife and drop into boiling water. Just before the water reaches the second boil, remove the kombo and set aside (the water will be used again in niban dashi). Reduce the heat and stir the katsuo-bushi into the water. Remove the saucepan from the heat. Strain the stock through a sieve lined with a cotton or muslin cloth. Set the katsuo-bushi aside (they will also be used to make niban dashi).

stock (dashi)

The method and ingredients for making stock differ according to requirements. Stock that is the base for a clear soup must, necessarily, be more carefully seasoned than one that is to be used for cooking vegetables. High quality kelp (kombo) and bonito shavings (katsuo-bushi) are essential for making delicious stocks.

A note on quantities –

For a sushi main course, count on the following quantities for each person:

- 200 g of uncooked rice
- 2–3 sheets of nori, fewer if you are making mostly nigiri
- 225 g fish or vegetable filling
- Have full bottles of vinegar and soy sauce, and a few spoonfuls of wasabi, and you shouldn't run out.

niban dashi:
stock for cooking vegetables and miso soup

method

Combine the kombo and katsuo-bushi left over from the ichiban dashi in a saucepan with the 200 ml of water. Place the pan over a high heat. Just before the water reaches the full boil remove the kombo. Lower the heat. Simmer over a gentle heat until about twenty per cent of the water has evaporated. Strain the stock through a sieve lined with a cotton cloth.

purchasing fresh fish

You can use almost any fish for sushi, so long as it is very fresh, preferably straight from the market that morning.

Some fish for sushi are usually served raw, while other varieties are normally cooked. Popular raw fish choices include:

- Turbot (Hirame)
- Tuna (maguro, or the fattier toro)
- Sea bass (suzuki)
- Mackerel (saba)
- Salmon (sake).

We will discuss some of the best fish for sushi a little later on in this book.

guidelines to picking fresh fish

A fish which has been left sitting in a shop for a few days is easily distinguished from a healthy, fresh fish. The inexperienced shopper just needs to remember a few simple guidelines while making their purchase.

The eyes of a fresh fish should be clear and bright. The gills should be red, not a dull brown, while the overall appearance should be shiny and wet and the flesh firm. Reject any fish that looks dry, and has soft flesh which is pulpy to touch. Your nose will tell you the rest – a fresh fish smells of the sea. If the smell is unpleasant or pungent, don't buy it.

Unless you are preparing sushi for a large group of people, you will be buying fish already gutted and filleted. In this case, the obvious indicators of freshness such as the eyes will have been removed, but you can tell from looking at a fillet whether it is fresh enough to use. Once again, the key thing to look for is dryness.

A freshly cut fillet should still have a shiny surface, and the grain in the flesh should not have begun to ridge or come apart from dryness on the surface. Of course, some fishmongers will wet fish down with water, but this will not stop the fish from beginning to come apart, and the flesh will lose its firmness if watered too regularly after being filleted.

Even when you are sure the fish you have bought is fresh, storing it properly until use is important. Unwrap it and wash it before re-wrapping it tightly in clingfilm, and always keep it at the bottom of the refrigerator.

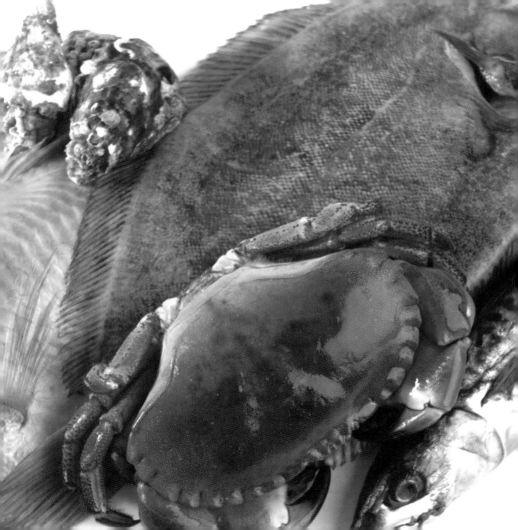

choosing fish
for sushi

- **karei** (lemon sole)
- **katsuo** (bonito)
- **maguro** (bluefin tuna)
- **saba** (mackerel)
- **sake** (salmon)
- **tai** (red snapper, sea bream)
- **ohyo garei** (halibut)
- **hirame** (turbot)
- **hirame** (brill)

karei (lemon sole)

Although it is a type of flounder, the lemon sole is regarded as part of the 'karei' family group.

This fish, with its succulent texture, is quite underrated as a sushi delicacy. It has a unique flavour, almost sweet and very delicate, and is very popular outside Japan.

The back fillets are best for sushi, being slightly thicker and easier to slice.

katsuo (bonito)

Bonito actually belongs to the mackerel family but is also related to the tuna, and is sometimes known as the skipjack tuna.

Very popular in Japan, it migrates northwards along the Japanese coast, and fresh bonito is usually available there in May. It is caught with a single rod to prevent damage to its flesh and is a very fast swimmer.

Outside Japan, the rest of the world is reliant on the bonito fished off the coast of North America, but unfortunately it doesn't freeze well. Fresh bonito is normally lightly grilled and then submerged in cold water. The flesh is a deep rosy colour and has a very rich, distinctive flavour.

For those of us unable to obtain fresh bonito, there is a ready supply of dried flakes, shaved from the flesh of the fish, available in Japanese food shops and some supermarkets.

Wonderful in sushi and a staple ingredient of dashi sushi, bonito is often served with ginger.

maguro (bluefin tuna)

The Bluefin tuna is one of the largest bony fishes. Found all over the world in temperate and subtropical waters, tuna has become one of the most popular ingredients of sushi.

It is classified as a red meat fish in Japan and divided into different pieces, graded by fat content. Tuna has a soft, meaty texture, which could be identified as rare roast beef.

As it does not taste exceptionally fishy, it is a great introduction for the sushi novice. The tastiest part of the tuna is known as 'toro' – the fatty part of the tuna belly, prized for its melt-in-the-mouth texture and subtle flavour. It is also the most expensive cut.

Other cuts include the meat around the spine which is very lean (the least popular), steaks cut from the back or the tail, and cuts from the upper part of the tuna, which are very rich in flavour.

shime sabe
ingredients

- 4 x 150 g mackerel fillets
- 8 tablespoons sea salt
- 500 ml su
- 2 tablespoons mirin

method

Using a large bowl, pour salt over the mackerel fillets, ensuring that each one is well covered. Drain the fillets for about an hour in a colander to make sure the juices drain well. Rinse under cold water and pat dry. Mix the su and mirin, and add the mackerel making sure the fillets are immersed. Allow to marinate for at least an hour. Then remove and pat dry and gently peel off the skin, starting at the top. Check for bones by running your fingers up and down the fillet, removing any you find with plastic tweezers.

saba (mackerel)

Saba is a rich and oily fish, with a very strong flavour that does not suit all tastes, perhaps explaining why it is not as popular as other fish.

High in protein and rich in beneficial oils, it is best fished in winter and must be frozen immediately to protect its freshness and quality. The skin is very thin, almost like parchment, and must be removed as it may harbour bacteria.

Normally served with hand-rolled sushi, saba is best when salted and marinated, which makes it very tender and much easier to slice.

The flavour will vary depending on the marinade used – most sushi chefs will have their own distinctive recipe.

sake (salmon)

Salmon is perhaps the most easily recognised fish in a sushi dish. It has a vibrant, orange colour and tastes wonderful. Treasured as a delicious and tender treat by many cultures, sadly wild salmon are rapidly becoming endangered, only plentiful in the Pacific.

Only salmon caught at sea are considered suitable for sushi by the discerning chef, and they are never served raw in sushi bars due to the potential presence of parasites in the fish. Sometimes lightly grilled and sometimes cured with salt and vinegar, salmon will never taste the same from one sushi bar to the next.

Despite the general disparagement shown to farm-raised salmon, conditions are gradually improving and it is much cheaper to buy. They are generally more tender to eat and have a higher fat content. They are also considered to be healthier to eat because of the presence of more unsaturated fatty acids – Omega 3 and 6.

When buying farm salmon, look for 'tagged' salmon, which comes from farms with better conditions. Despite this, however, wild salmon is still considered superior in every way!

Don't try serving raw salmon at home. Curing the salmon reduces the dangers of parasite infection in the fish, and also removes moisture from the flesh, resulting in firm and supple meat. The added process of freezing the fish at very low temperatures should ensure that the salmon is completely safe to eat. We have included a basic curing recipe for you to try at home.

cured salmon
ingredients

- Fresh salmon, filleted or whole
- Sea salt
- White wine or rice vinegar

method

Place the salmon in a shallow box and rub both sides thoroughly with sea salt. Place in the refrigerator and leave for about an hour. Remove and immediately rinse, thoroughly, with cold water and pat dry with a paper towel. Soak in white wine or rice vinegar for no longer than twenty minutes, removing any of the outer layer which may be discoloured and tough from the marinade. Freeze for at least four days. Defrost when required and use immediately.

Note: The word for rice wine and salmon sound very similar and are spelt exactly the same: 'sake'. In case you are worried about ordering wine instead of fish, remember to say 'sah-kay' for rice wine and 'sha-kay' for salmon!

tai (red snapper, sea bream)

Although tai, translated as 'sea bream,' appears on standard sushi menus, a substitute fish is often used in its place as it is not available everywhere. Raw tai has a character and flavour all of its own, making it a very popular sushi selection in Japan. It is considered to be the most noble fish in the ocean by the Japanese and demand for it far exceeds supply. The firm flesh is pink and white and the flavour is very delicate. Although not available outside Japan, it has many close cousins and these are often used as substitutes, the best being the red snapper.

ohyo garei (halibut)

Halibut are flat fish from the 'karei' family, so called because they have eyes on the right of the head.

They spend a lot of time on the floor of the ocean and can grow as long as 4 metres. When caught, it puts up a good fight and has large, powerful jaws. As the fish ages, its dense and meaty flesh can lose some of its excellent flavour so it is best to use younger fish for sushi. They do become oilier and more succulent during the winter and are mainly sold in steak form outside Japan.

hirame (turbot)

The word 'hirame' refers to flat fish with eyes on the left of their head, as opposed to 'karei' which are flat fish with eyes on the right of their head.

Of all hirame, the turbot is considered to be the most prestigious by all sushi lovers: exquisitely flavoured flesh with a meaty, succulent texture. Best eaten raw, the edge of the fillet is slightly crunchy and is considered to be a delicacy – ask your fishmonger not to remove it and try the taste yourself. Although farmed turbot is gradually becoming more widely available, turbot are still plentiful in the wild.

hirame (brill)

Often served as 'hirame', this is a pale imitation of its excellent cousin, the turbot. It is the least popular of the hirame family for sushi dishes, having a bland watery flavour which belies its firm meaty flesh.

The wisest move when ordering hirame is to ask the sushi chef the name of the fish in English. This may prevent disappointment if you are expecting a treat.

If you would like to try this at home, buy a back fillet as it has more meat.

fish preparation

preparing fish

When handling a fish, always hold it by the head or tail to keep the flesh firm, and always use a sharp knife. There is a common saying that 'a sharp knife is a safe knife', the theory behind this being the less you have to struggle, or force the knife, the less likely it is that there will be an accident.

scaling the fish

Begin to prepare the fish by firstly washing it in cool running water to remove any slime. Dampening the fish will also make scaling easier. Not all fish need scaling. If you're not sure, run the blade of a blunt knife at almost a 90-degree angle to the body from tail-end to head. If the scales are thick and come up easily, you need to remove them.

Hold down the head of the fish firmly with your left hand. Moving from head to tail, scrape off the scales with a knife in your right hand. Repeat the process on

the other side of the fish and continue until the body is smooth.

gutting the fish

Place the head of the fish to the left with the belly toward you. Lift up the pectoral fin (bottom fin of the fish) and using a sharp knife, drive the blade point into the vent (small anal opening near the tail, where the body begins opening near the tail, where the body begins to widen). Cut right through the belly all the way to the gills. Remove the guts from the cavity. Use a spoon and scoop out the dark reddish-brown kidney line that lies along the backbone.

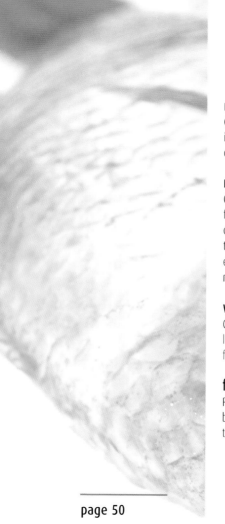

removing the head and tail

Cut the head off below the gills and the tail where it joins the body. It is important to cut out **ALL** parts of the gills.

removing the dorsal fin bones

Cut along the length of each side of the dorsal fin (top) of the fish. Remove the dorsal fin and connected bones by giving a quick pull from tail-end to head. This step is not essential, but eliminates those tiny, annoying bones that can ruin a meal.

washing the fish

Clean the fish in salted water, especially the cavity left behind by the removal of the entrails. Wipe the fish dry with a clean cloth.

filleting a fish

Place the fish diagonally on a cutting board with the belly facing right and the tail towards you. Cut from the pelvic fin towards the tail. Turn the fish over.

Insert the knife through the back, so that the blade grazes the ribcage, and cut from right to left, all the way to the tail.

Turn the fish at 180 degrees. With the point of the knife, cut through the bones which form the top of the ribcage. Separate the fillet from the body. Turn the fish over, bone side down, and cut the meat free from the backbone, slicing from the tail to the head. Turn the fish 180 degrees. Cut the meat at the base of the tail free from the backbone. Separate the fillet from the body. Cut out the bones of the ribcage still attached to the fillet.

removing the skin

Place the fillet on a cutting board, with the tail to the left and the skin side down. Make a cut at the base of the tail-end. Grip the skin of the tail with your left hand, insert the knife with your right hand between the skin and the meat, and with a sawing motion, pull the skin back over the blade, to separate the skin from the meat. Pull out any bones that are embedded with tweezers.

purchasing kai rui

general rules
Wash hands thoroughly before touching any type of shellfish. Shellfish should be kept cool and damp until required. Rinse if necessary to remove debris but avoid lengthy contact with fresh water. Do not subject the fish to drastic temperature changes. Keep it separately from other foods and prevent contamination by using clean containers and utensils for storage, preparation and serving.

guidelines to picking kai rui (shellfish and roe)
In the best of all possible worlds, certain shellfish such as oysters, crab, lobster, prawn and abalone should be purchased live for use in sushi. In general this is not always practical. We have included a few general guidelines which will help you to choose the most fresh and best seafood from a licensed reputable fishmonger.

hotate gai (scallops), kaki oysters and awabi
Abalone Scallops, oysters and abalone should be bought when their shells are tightly closed to be sure they are alive. They should not float in water and should feel heavy. Do not choose this type of shellfish if the shell is chipped. Abalone is a protected species in the wild so ensure that any you purchase have a yellow tag to indicate that they have been farmed. Fresh scallops will have a distinctive sweet smell when fresh.

ebi (prawn)

Fresh prawns can prove difficult to find. If you do come across fresh prawn for sale, check them carefully before buying. They should be firm, with tight-fitting shells with clear, distinctive markings, and should smell fresh. If even one in a batch smells slightly of ammonia, the whole batch is likely to be unsuitable for purchase.

tako (octopus)

If buying a whole octopus, check that the eyes are not cloudy, but clear and bright. The octopus should smell like the ocean and not fishy, and should look shiny and firm. If the tentacles and skin are intact this is a good sign showing that the octopus has been handled carefully. High quality frozen octopus is much better than poor quality fresh octopus, so bear this in mind.

preparing kai rui

ebi (prawns)

The most popular sushi dishes contain prawns in one form or another. Scavengers by nature, prawns inhabit salt and brackish fresh water, and are mostly found on shallow seafloors, where they feed on small animals and plants. In Japan ama ebi (raw prawn) is considered one of the greatest sushi delicacies, having a beautiful translucent appearance and tasting very sweet.

The safest approach is to buy frozen prawns and drop them into boiling water to ensure they are cooked before eating. Cooked prawns are referred to as ebi – the firm, striped pink and white flesh is a delicious treat for both the seasoned and uninitiated sushi gourmet.

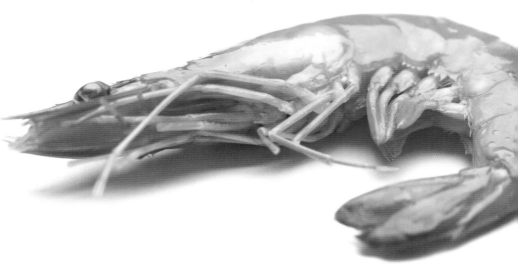

preparation

To prepare prawns the first step is to de-vein the fish properly and then skewer the body on a cocktail stick without removing the shell. This will prevent curling of the body while it is cooking. Add a dash of rice vinegar to boiling water before dropping in the prawns. Allow to boil for about three minutes or until the flesh is opaque and pink. Remove and immediately plunge into cold water. Carefully remove the cocktail stick and peel off the shells, leaving the tails for decoration.

Split each down the underside, taking care not to cut all the way through. Spread open into a butterfly shape and use as an effective topping.

awabi (abalone)

Abalone is one of the most expensive sushi toppings and is cultivated commercially in Japan to meet the huge local demand. Prized for its mother-of-pearl inner shell and the unique flavour of its foot, abalone can grow up to 30 cm wide – however the larger the abalone, the more rubbery the flesh! The meat part of an abalone can be as much as 2 cm thick and as large as the size of a hand, ranging in colour from pale peach to grey. Often displayed in a shell when presented for sushi, it is best served with a little soy sauce on the side. Much tougher when cooked, abalone is usually served raw and very thinly sliced across the grain.

preparation

Open the shell by sliding a short, strong knife under the foot in the shell and cut through the muscle. Remove the intestines and wipe the remainder of the meat clean. Remove the mouth and the dark fringe and discard. Wash the meat under cold running water, scrubbing off any mucous with a brush. Using a very sharp knife, slice very thinly across the grain and score slightly to tenderise the meat.

hotate-gai (scallops)

Delicately flavoured, raw slices of scallops are commonly used as a topping for temaki or uramaki sushi. Generally available at fishmongers, they need to be refrigerated immediately after capture if they are to be sold fresh. However, scallops do freeze well, without loss of flavour.

The muscle which is normally eaten is creamy white in colour, sometimes slightly orange as a result of the algae consumed. Served raw, it is perhaps preferred by the more seasoned sushi diner.

preparation

Open the shell by sliding a short, strong knife into the shell and, keeping the blade flat, slice through the muscle which attaches the upper and lower shells. Once the shell is open, sever the muscle completely. Tear off the orange fringe and any coral and discard, preserving only the white meat. Rinse under cold running water and then slice thinly across the top of the scallop. Use immediately.

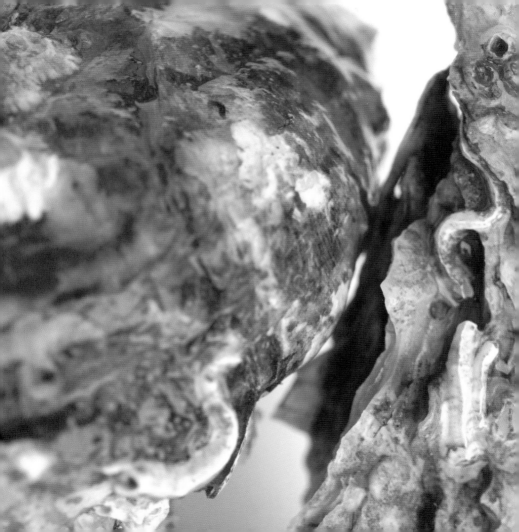

kaki (oysters)

Revered by all gourmets as the greatest dining experience, the oyster is famed all over the world as a gastronomic delight. Eaten raw and whole, the meat has a light, salty flavour and is generally used as a topping for gunkan maki. This form of sushi is made by rolling a wide piece of nori around formed sushi rice, making sure there is a gap between the top of the rice and the nori. The oyster is then pressed onto the rice and is contained by the nori. As the grey body is quite watery, oysters are not really suitable for any other form of sushi.

preparation

Oyster shells can be quite difficult to pry apart. The best method is to place the oyster on a firm surface, using a cloth to protect your hand from the sharp barnacles often found on the shell. Push the knife into the narrowest point of the shell and twist it to separate the two parts of the shell. Insert the knife, keeping it flat against the upper shell and then slice from side to side to cut the muscle. Remove the upper shell and then remove the muscle from the lower shell. Rinse under running water and use immediately.

kani (crab)

Crab is not traditionally used in Japanese sushi. However, in most sushi bars in the western world, crab will be on the menu in one form or another. Do not be fooled by crab sticks – they contain absolutely no crab meat at all. The best flavoured meat comes from the Alaskan King crab, unfortunately not common worldwide! Crab meat is always served cooked for sushi but, if cooked from frozen, the meaty white flesh can taste a bit bland. Many people balk at buying a live crab and the difficult and lengthy preparation process to extract the white meat used for sushi. The best option is to buy a dressed crab, which is more readily available.

preparation

Assuming you have bought a dressed crab, choose the whitest meat and flake it, checking for any bits of shell which may not have been removed. The brown meat is too strongly flavoured for sushi and unless you are going to use it for something else, it should be discarded at this point. The sweetest and best white meat comes from the claws of both male and female, and from the apron found under the body of the female crab. Use as soon as possible and keep refrigerated away from other foods, until required.

tako (octopus)

Easily identified on the sushi menu, the octopus feeds on many other sushi ingredients, such as crab and lobster, which provides a high protein diet and results in an excellent flavour when cooked. Always cooked, the meat has a firm texture and the thick tentacles, the only part of the octopus used for sushi, make a great topping for hand-formed sushi. The surprising transformation of the skin from dull grey to burgundy during the cooking process is remarkable. Slightly chewy and rubbery, the clean, subtle flavour will appeal to almost everyone.

preparation

Although an octopus can be eaten raw, only the cooked tentacles are used for sushi. If you have a fresh, whole octopus, remove the tentacles from just below the eye. Rub the flesh with salt before cooking to clean and tenderise the flesh. Clean the suckers and ends to remove any sand or grit. Add salt to boiling water and add the tentacles. Once the water is boiling again, reduce the heat and simmer gently for about ten minutes. Drain and allow to cool. Cut away the central section which contains the mouth parts and discard. Slice diagonally to reveal the pure white meat inside.

fish roe

Most types of fish roe are served in gunkan maki sushi as they are distinctly unmanageable and difficult to contain in a normal sushi roll. Ikura (salmon roe) is best presented in this way and is quite familiar in sushi bars. Sometimes called red caviar, the large eggs are bright orange and very tasty.

An exception is flying fish roe, which has much smaller eggs and is often used as a coating to add colour to uramaki (inside-out sushi rolls).

Also very common in sushi bars, it has a characteristic bright, orange colour and tiny eggs, which are flavoursome, firm and salty.

Most types of roe are available in processed form, either salted or cured. Occasionally fresh roe is available, normally having been gently marinated in sake and soy sauce ensuring a less salty flavour. The various types of roe come in an array of beautiful colours, ranging from red to gold, and the intriguing flavours and textures tingle in the mouth when eaten.

preparing the other ingredients

Generally you should prepare ingredients as close to the serving time of the food as possible.

Use a very sharp, non-serrated kitchen knife to cut sushi ingredients and maki rolls. Cut fish and seafood across the grain, at about a 30-degree angle. Try to avoid a sawing motion when you slice into raw fish; the cuts should be made cleanly, without tearing the flesh.

Slice one kind of fish at a time, and then wrap it in clingfilm and refrigerate until you're ready to assemble the sushi. Wash your cutting board and knife each time you finish slicing an ingredient.

In addition to fish, you may also use tamago (or omelette). See recipes for different types of omelette on pages 24–25.

nigiri preparation

The slice of fish or omelette for nigiri is roughly rectangular in shape, and 6 cm long by about 2 cm wide. Slice tender fish about 7 mm thick; firm fish about 3 mm.

maki preparation

Cut fish or seafood, omelette, seedless cucumber, Japanese pickle, reconstituted dried shiitake mushrooms, or avocado into long, thin strips that are about 4 cm in length. You can also use trimmings from your nigiri ingredient preparation.

preparing the rice

Perfect sushi rice must be sticky enough to hold nigiri pieces and maki rolls together, and its vinegar seasoning is a delicately balanced mixture of sour, sweet and salty. The following are general guidelines for cooking and dressing it.

Nothing is more important to the sushi experience than the taste of the rice. This is where the skill of the sushi chef comes into play, and separates one from the other. Selecting the highest quality ingredients is the best way to start.

Once you have bought some good rice, the next problem is to cook it to perfection. It is not as difficult as you would expect, but it is an exacting process which once mastered, will almost guarantee perfect rice.

nori preparation

Cut the nori for your sushi rolls in half lengthwise with a pair of scissors. In a small bowl, mix water and a little rice vinegar (su). This is used for moistening your hands so rice doesn't stick to them. It can also be used to bind the nori in tricky situations.

If your wasabi is not already prepared, mix some with water in a little bowl to form a thick paste. You will not need more than a few spoonfuls, as it's fiery hot.

water

The amount of water you use depends on the kind of rice you are using. Too little will result in rice that is dry and hard in the centre, too much will produce rice that is soupy.

rice

150 g of raw rice yields about 450 g of cooked rice. If you're making maki, count on up to 150 g of cooked rice per roll or for six to eight pieces. If you're making nigiri, count on about one-fifth that amount per piece.

method

Soak the rice for one hour before cooking. Next, wash the rice by rubbing between the palms of your hands. This will remove any bran or polishing compound that remains. Drain off the old water and add fresh water. Repeat this step until the water becomes clear.

Combine the rice and the measured amount of water (one part rice with one-and-a-half parts water) in a saucepan and cover. Place the pan over a moderately high heat. As soon as the water boils, reduce the heat and cook for twenty minutes. Turn off the heat and allow the rice to steam, undisturbed, for at least ten minutes. Do not remove the lid during the cooking process. The briefest look will let out steam and ruin the rice. While the rice is cooking you should prepare the dressing.

vinegar dressing

If you don't have seasoned rice vinegar, combine four

parts unseasoned rice vinegar with two parts sugar and one part salt. Stir rapidly until the sugar and salt have dissolved in the vinegar. Adjust the sugar and salt to taste.

Count on one or two tablespoons of dressing for every 150 g of cooked rice.

This is a good basic recipe. It will give you an excellent start on devising a recipe with different proportions that suits your own taste. The best way to start customising the recipe is to adjust the amount of sugar. However, too much sugar will not go well with any finger sushi that contains raw fish.

blending

Put the hot, cooked rice into a moistened wooden, ceramic, or plastic mixing bowl, and spoon the dressing over the top, one tablespoon at a time. Gently cut through the rice with a wooden or plastic spoon, or spatula, to mix the dressing and rice evenly. Taste it occasionally to check the vinegar. Straight after you combine the rice with the dressing, start cooling the rice to room temperature. As you mix, cut, turn, and fan the rice to cool it. Fanning the rice will give it a glossy, pearly lustre. Gently turn the rice in the bowl and fan it energetically until it is cool to the touch; this should take about 5–10 minutes.

storing the rice before use

The rice is now ready for use. When you prepare the other sushi ingredients, store the prepared rice in its bowl on the counter, with a damp, clean tea towel covering the top of the bowl. Don't put it in the refrigerator to cool or store – refrigeration hardens the rice, and the cold dulls the delicate flavour of the dressing.

serving sushi

presentation

On each serving dish (or in separate little bowls if you have lots of small serving dishes,) put a little mound of wasabi for guests to mix into their soy sauce.

Similarly, give them each a small spoonful of pickled ginger. Put out a bottle of soy sauce. Each diner should have a little dish for mixing the wasabi and soy sauce.

While chopsticks aren't necessary for eating, they are handy for stirring together wasabi and soy sauce and for picking up pieces of ginger. Give each guest a napkin or two (things can get a little messy).

Don't be disheartened if your nigiri and maki don't look very professional at the start. This is one art where rehearsal is truly its own reward.

drinks with sushi

drinks

Eating sushi is a very personal experience and, while you are eating and absorbing the fine delicate flavours, it can be very pleasant to enjoy a drink. Good sushi restaurants will offer a range of drinks, all chosen to enhance the sushi experience. None of the drinks discussed are difficult to obtain for use at home.

tea

Hot green tea, known as agari, is well known for cleansing the palate between tastes and also provides a gentle digestive aid.

sake

Sake flavour can range from dry to sweet and is normally served at room temperature. The alcohol content is quite high and even a small glass can provide quite a kick! Drinking sake is well known for its enhancement of the taste of sushi. It has a smooth, but understated, flavour and is commonly available.

beer

Most brands of beer go very well with sushi. It should always be served cold and its crisp, refreshing quality is well suited to the sushi experience.

wine

Choosing the correct wine to drink while eating sushi can be quite difficult. Some will choose the wine they prefer, regardless of the food to be consumed. In general, most light to medium white wines go well with fish and vegetables and a full-bodied white wine, such as Chardonnay, is fantastic with strongly flavoured fish. As a special touch when serving shellfish, a sparkling white wine or Champagne is an excellent choice.

nigiri sushi

You may not make perfectly formed nigiri on your first attempt, but your results should look presentable.

Sushi is served as it is made, so start assembling it when you and your guests are ready to eat.

prepare
Set rice, prepared nigiri toppings, wasabi paste, su, and serving plates on the worktop. Moisten your hands in the su, then shake or clap them once to get rid of extra water.

mould the rice
Each piece of nigiri should be a big mouthful, so scoop up about two tablespoons of rice. Gently press and shape it in your palm into an oval slightly smaller than your slices of fish.

suggested fish toppings
- Tako (octopus)
- Saba (mackerel)
- Maguro (tuna)
- Kani (crab)
- Ama-ebi (raw prawn)
- Ebi (cooked prawn)
- Kaibashira (scallops)
- Ikura (salmon roe)
- Ika (squid)
- Sake (salmon)
- Hirame (halibut)
- Unagi (freshwater eel)

position the fish

With your index finger, spread a dab of wasabi down the centre of a fish slice. Gently press the fish into the top of the rice, wasabi side down. The fish should droop a little over the ends of the rice oval. Place the formed nigiri on a serving plate, and make another of the same kind to serve with it.

Note: Some nigiri ingredients, including omelette, eel and some fish roe, are traditionally held onto the rice with a little strip of nori. If you're using these ingredients, cut the nori with scissors into strips 4 mm wide and 10 cm long. Lay the nori widthwise across the top of the nigiri and wrap the long ends under the bottom of the piece. Stick the ends together with a drop of su.

tamago yaki rice balls

ingredients

Prepared sushi rice •

Tamago Yaki •

method

Squeeze the vinegared rice together into the shape of an egg. Place an omelette piece over the top of the rice formation. Tie a piece of nori around the rice to hold the omelette piece in position.

smoked salmon and cucumber nigiri

Presentation is everything when arranging this dish. Practice makes perfect so don't despair if you can't get it right first-time round. It is worth persevering to master this most intricate dish. Preparation will take about thirty minutes and you will need a sushi mould.

method

Slice the salmon into thin strips and slice the cucumber lengthwise into narrow strips. Trim the salmon and cucumber to fit diagonally in the mould and then line the wet mould with alternating strips of salmon and cucumber. Add the rice and then place the lid on the mould and press gently to compress the contents.

Once removed from the mould, use a wet knife to cut into six equal pieces and serve.

ingredients

- Prepared sushi rice
- 100 g smoked salmon
- 15 cm length of cucumber
- Sushi mould, wet in advance

prawn sushi special

Not a traditional form of nigiri, more an adaptation, but tasty all the same.

ingredients

Prepared sushi rice ·

1 sheet nori ·

24 large prawns ·

2 teaspoons wasabi ·

method

Prepare the prawns by de-veining thoroughly, but leave the shells on. Insert a toothpick to prevent the body curling while being cooked. Boil some water in a pan, adding a dash of rice vinegar to the water. Drop the prawns into the water and boil for three minutes or until the flesh is pink and no longer transparent. Remove and plunge straight into cold water. Take out the toothpick and peel off the shell, leaving the tail for decoration.

Split each down the underside, taking care not to cut all the way through. Spread open into a butterfly shape. Gently shape the rice into oval balls. Dab a little wasabi paste onto the top of each ball and top with a prawn. Wrap a thin strip of nori around each oval and serve with wasabi paste, shoyu, and gari.

maki sushi

This type of sushi consists of fish or crab, and vegetables rolled in a sheet of nori and rice.

Usually served in bite-sized portions, it is an excellent introduction for a memorable first sushi experience, especially if you are a little squeamish about eating raw fish. The beauty of the presentation and the wonderful combination of salty seaweed, sweet rice and delicate fish and vegetables will win over the most reluctant diner. The rolls can be served with Japanese soy sauce presented in individual small, shallow bowls for easy dipping. Add more wasabi to the soy sauce for those who prefer a stronger taste.

Rolling maki sushi is slightly trickier to master than nigiri sushi, but once you become adept at the technique, you won't ever want to stop.

To make rolled sushi, rice is spread over a sheet of nori; fish and/or vegetables are laid across the rice; and the nori, rice, and filling are rolled together in a bamboo mat. The roll is then cut into bite-sized pieces and arranged on a plate, cut side up to show their filling.

prepare

Set the sushi mat down on the worktop in front of you, positioned so you can roll it away from you. Place half a sheet of nori, shiny side down, on top of the mat. Moisten your hands in su and clap or shake them once, to remove any excess moisture.

spread rice

Scoop up about 150 g of rice and place it on the nori. Gently spread it with your hands in a thin, even layer, leaving a 4 mm border of nori at the bottom and sides and a 16 mm border at the top.

fill

Take a little wasabi and spread it in a thin line across the centre of the rice, from one side to the other (omit the wasabi if you prefer). On top of the wasabi, lay strips of fish, vegetables, or omelette in a line. If you're using a half-sheet of nori, the filling should be no more than 12 mm thick.

roll

Lift the edge of the bamboo mat closest to you and fold it (and the rice-covered nori inside it) up over the filling in the middle. Think of the mat and nori as a small wave breaking over the top of the filling. When the rice-covered nori touches down on the other side of the filling, the rice will adhere to the rice and nori sheet.

If you're using a half-sheet, this one fold will probably have met the top edge of the nori, and you'll have a cylinder of sushi.

If there's more rice and nori showing at the top of the

mat, keep hold of the edge of the bamboo mat. Don't tuck it under the roll, but keep guiding it parallel to the mat so it keeps a U-shaped curve. Press your other hand lightly on top of the curve of the mat as you roll the sushi cylinder over the remaining nori.

When the nori is all rolled up and stuck together, unroll the mat so it lies flat with the sushi cylinder on top of it. Then re-roll the mat around the sushi cylinder. Encircle the mat-wrapped cylinder with a hand at either end, squeeze gently, and hold for a few seconds. This solidifies the roll. Unroll the mat, and place the sushi cylinder on a cutting board.

slice

As with all rolled sushi, you can either leave the ends trimmed or not, depending on who you are serving the sushi to! If you are going to trim the ends, do this first and discard or eat the trimmings. Now cut the cylinder in half, and slice each half into three or four pieces of equal size. Arrange on a small serving plate.

filling suggestions:

- De-seeded cucumber with sesame seeds
- Red pepper
- Shiitake mushroom
- Avocado and salmon
- Carrot and coriander
- Omelette and chive
- Raw tuna
- Finely-chopped tuna, green onion and chilli pepper
- Cooked eel and cucumber

sushi beef and spinach

ingredients

Prepared sushi rice ·

Nori ·

225 g beef fillet ·

570 g spinach leaves, ·
finely sliced

3 tablespoons sour cream ·

30 ml lemon juice ·

1 tablespoon shoyu ·

2 tablespoons olive oil ·

1 tablespoon canola oil ·

Wasabi ·

Coarse sea salt ·

Mixed peppercorns ·

method

Slice the spinach very finely and put aside in a bowl. Preheat a frying pan until it is very hot. Cover the beef with oil, roll in salt and cover all sides well with peppercorns. Brown the beef off in the hot oil. Remove from heat and allow to stand for ten minutes, then slice thinly.

Mix the lemon juice, shoyu, and olive oil with a fork, whisking well, and pour over the spinach. At this stage, mix a little wasabi (to taste) into the sour cream and put aside.

Dampen hands. Cut a nori sheet in half and place rice on the lower half. Drape a few slices of beef on the rice and then decorate with spinach salad in a diagonal pattern. Shake some of the wasabi and sour cream mixture over the salad and then roll, moistening the top edge to seal the roll. Repeat the process until the ingredients are finished.

tekka-maki (raw tuna roll)

ingredients
Prepared sushi rice ·

4 sheets nori ·

100 g raw tuna ·

method
Cut the tuna into thin strips. Place a sheet of nori on the makisu (sushi mat). Spread the rice over the nori, leaving borders as described on page 82. Place the tuna strips lengthwise on the rice and roll.

red pepper and mushroom rolls

ingredients

- Prepared sushi rice
- 4 sheets nori
- 2 large mushrooms
- 2 red peppers
- 8 spring onions

method

Grill the spring onions with some olive oil and season to taste. Place to one side. Grill the mushrooms and peppers, and season with salt and pepper. As soon as the mushrooms and peppers are cool, slice them into long, thick strips. Place a sheet of nori, shiny side down, on a sushi mat and lightly pat on 8 cm of rice on the bottom half, up to 2.5 cm thick.

Place the mushrooms, peppers, and green onions, over two-thirds of the bottom end of rice. Roll the mat, moistening the end and allow to rest before cutting in equal pieces and serving.

tuna and beef kimbob

Although the preparation, approach and final display of Korean kimbob rolls are very similar to maki sushi, they normally contain cooked meat. We have included a couple of recipes for you to try.

method

Dice the onion and slice the cucumber, spinach, and carrot into thin strips. Put aside. Whisk the eggs with one tablespoon of shoyu and the water. Pour into a frying pan and cook until thickened over a medium heat. Remove from heat, allow to cool and cut into strips. Heat the oil and slowly cook the onion until tender. Add the beef and the rest of the shoyu and cook until evenly brown. Drain the juices and put the mixture aside.

Preheat the oven to 350°F/180°C/Gas Mark 4. Heat the nori on a baking sheet for 1–2 minutes, until slightly crisp. Place the nori sheets, one at a time, on a bamboo rolling mat. Line the nori sheets evenly with the rice, taking care not to let the rice cover the edges of the nori. Beginning at one end of the nori sheet, place a stick of carrot, a line of tuna, a cucumber slice and a line of beef on the rice. Repeat until the food reaches approximately the middle of the nori sheet. Roll the sheets carefully, cut and serve.

ingredients

- Prepared sushi rice
- 6 sheets nori
- 350 g ground beef, lean
- 1 tin tuna chunks in brine, drained
- 1 onion
- 1 cucumber
- 1 carrot
- Spinach leaves
- 2 eggs
- 2 tablespoons shoyu
- 1 tablespoon vegetable oil
- 3 tablespoons water

beef and vegetable kimbob

This is not an easy kimbob roll to master and you will need lots of preparation time. It is a very popular sushi dish and the time spent will be worth the effort.

method

Add three tablespoons of sesame oil and one tablespoon of sesame seed salt to the cooked rice. Mix in well and allow to cool. Mix in the beef, sugar, garlic powder, sesame seed salt, shoyu and dashida and let the mixture marinate for about two hours. Slice the carrots thinly and gently fry in a little oil along with the marinated beef mixture, for about two minutes. Slice the spinach finely. Mix the lemon juice, shoyu, and olive oil with a fork, whisking well and pour over the spinach. Beat and season the eggs and fry over a medium heat until firm. Fold each side inwards, top over first, then bottom over. It will end up about one-third of its original size. Once it is cool, cut into narrow strips which are the length of the nori. Slice the pepper in the same way.

Keep a bowl of water handy to wet your fingers when needed. Place the rice over two-thirds of the nori sheet, and then begin laying your ingredients over the rice. Place a row of spinach, egg, beef, carrot, and pepper crosswise. Moisten your fingers with water when they become sticky. Start rolling the nori from the end closest to you. Gently squeeze to tighten the roll. Place the roll seam side down and let it rest for a few minutes before cutting into thick slices.

ingredients

- Prepared sushi rice
- 5-6 sheets nori
- 450 g ground beef, lean
- 2 carrots
- Spinach leaves
- Red pepper
- 3 eggs
- 1 tablespoon sugar
- 1 teaspoon garlic powder
- 1 teaspoon sesame seed salt
- 3 tablespoons shoyu
- 1 teaspoon dashida (Korean beef stock)
- 3 tablespoons seasame oil
- 1 tablespoon canola oil

futomaki

Futomaki is a larger version of a maki roll, which uses the same technique to roll, just on a larger scale.

method

Arrange all your chosen ingredients and moisten your hands with su before beginning to roll the sushi. Place the nori on top of the mat and add an even layer of rice. Arrange your choice of fillings in a line, as with a maki roll, but bear in mind that the roll is meant to be bigger and thicker once rolled.

Once the nori has been rolled over, press your other hand lightly on top of the curve of the mat as you roll the sushi cylinder over the remaining nori.

When the nori is all rolled up and stuck together, unroll the mat so it lies flat with the sushi cylinder on top of it. Then re-roll the mat around the sushi cylinder, pushing any loose ingredients and rice back into each end. Squeeze and unroll the mat, and place the sushi on a cutting board, cut in half and slice each half into three or four pieces of equal size.

filling suggestions:
- Carrots
- Red pepper
- Avocado
- Chives
- Cucumber
- Omelette
- Fresh Tuna
- Salmon
- Prawns
- Cooked spinach
- Kampyo
- Crab meat
- Mayonnaise
- Asparagus
- Fried tofu

vegetarian futomaki

ingredients

Prepared sushi rice ·

6 sheets nori ·

Spinach leaves ·

4 large dried shiitake ·
mushrooms (soaked
in warm water)

4 ribbons kampyo ·
(dried gourd)

500 ml dashi ·
(vegetable stock)

3 eggs ·

2 teaspoons sugar ·

Salt to taste ·

Shoyu ·

1 tablespoon mirin ·

preparation

Boil the spinach leaves until wilted. Beat the eggs, one teaspoon of sugar, dashi and salt together. Heat some oil in a frying pan and pour in the egg mixture to make an omelette. Once it has set, slide it onto a plate and cut into 12 mm wide slices. Boil the mushrooms and kampyo in the dashi, adding one teaspoon of shoyu, the mirin, one teaspoon sugar, and salt to taste. Slice the mushrooms into strips. The kampyo should be sliced into strips the same length as the nori sheets.

method

Lay your bamboo rolling mat on a flat work surface. Place a sheet of nori on the mat and cover two-thirds with a thin layer of rice. Wetting fingers in vinegar water will help to smooth the rice evenly. Place a strip of egg, a strip of spinach, and the strips of mushroom across the width of the nori and a strip of kampyo on top of the rice nearest to you. Carefully roll the sushi to stop the ingredients sliding around. Once you have made all the rolls, cut each one into inch thick slices.

crab and herbs sushi salad

For a delicious combination, serve with Prawn Tempura – on page 100.

method

Using a fork, mix the honey, lemon juice, mustard and oil together. Add the herbs, crab, and onion and season to taste. Place the nori, matt side upwards, on a sushi mat. Cover the lower half with a thick layer of rice. Cover two-thirds of the rice with the crab filling before gently rolling into shape. Remembering to moisten the ends to seal the edges properly. Cut equal-sized pieces and serve.

ingredients

- Prepared sushi rice
- 4 sheets nori
- 1 small onion, very finely sliced
- 450 g fresh crab
- A handful of chopped parsley
- A handful of chopped basil
- $\frac{1}{2}$ tablespoon honey
- $\frac{1}{2}$ tablespoon lemon juice
- $\frac{1}{2}$ tablespoon mustard
- $\frac{1}{2}$ tablespoon canola oil
- Salt and pepper to taste

prawn tempura

method

To make the prawn tempura:

Peel and de-vein the prawns. Combine the flour, egg, and ice water to make a batter, keeping back a little flour on a separate plate. Score the prawns across the back and press down to elongate. Preheat some vegetable or peanut oil in a frying pan. Check the heat by dropping in a little batter – if it floats back to the surface, the temperature should be fine. Coat the prawns in batter and fry quickly.

To make the roll:

Mix the crab meat with a little mayonnaise and add the hot sauce to taste. Add a layer of rice over a sheet of nori. Spread a layer of cream cheese over the rice and add the crab meat mixture, thinly sliced cucumber, sliced radish sprouts, and avocado slices. Lay two prawn pieces across. Roll, cut, and serve as usual.

ingredients

- Prepared sushi rice
- 2 sheets of nori
- Large prawns – 2 per roll
- 30 g crab meat
- ½ cucumber
- Kiware radish sprouts
- 1 avocado
- 3 teaspoons cream cheese
- 110 g flour
- 1 egg
- 235 ml iced water
- Mayonnaise
- Sriracha Hot Sauce or chilli sauce

californian roll

ingredients

- Prepared sushi rice
- 2 sheets nori
- Crab meat
- Natural ginger, thinly sliced
- 1 cucumber
- 1 ripe avocado
- Mayonnaise

method

Slice the ginger, cucumber, and avocado into thin slices. Mix a little mayonnaise with the crab meat to help it bind before preparing in the normal way.

sweet californian roll

method

Combine the honey, sesame seeds, sesame oil, and mayonnaise together to make a smooth sesame sauce. Mix the tuna, sugar, and shoyu together and simmer on a low heat for five minutes. Spread the rice on a nori sheet and coat with the sesame sauce. Once cool, arrange the tuna mixture, crab sticks and cucumber sticks as desired. Roll and serve as usual.

ingredients

- Prepared sushi rice
- 2 sheets nori
- 1 can drained tuna
- Imitation crab sticks
- 1 cucumber, cut into thin strips
- 4-5 heaped tablespoons mayonnaise
- 4 teaspoons honey
- $\frac{1}{2}$ tablespoon sesame oil
- 2 tablespoons sugar
- 2 tablespoons shoyu
- 4 teaspoons toasted sesame seeds

boston roll

ingredients

Prepared sushi rice ·

2 sheets nori ·

200 g fresh tuna ·

Lettuce sliced into ·
thin strips

1 ripe avocado, ·
sliced into thin strips

method

The tuna can be flaked or sliced into thin strips.
Slice the avocado and lettuce thinly as well and
lay the ingredients across the rice and nori
sheet, before rolling and cutting.

philadelphia roll

Also known as the roll of brotherly love, this roll gets its name from the cream cheese applied to the insides. For an added special flavour, you can use sliced avocado and smelt eggs.

ingredients

- Prepared sushi rice
- 2 sheets nori
- 30 g mildly flavoured smoked salmon,
- ½ cucumber
- 3-4 tablespoons cream cheese

method

De-seed the cucumber and slice, along with the salmon, into very thin strips. Spread a layer of rice over the nori as normal before lining with the cream cheese. Add the other ingredients as normal but omit adding, or serving with wasabi as it will mask the delicate flavours of the other ingredients.

soft-shelled crab rolls

method

Preheat the oil in a deep pan until it is very hot. Coat the crabs in flour and fry each one for about thirty seconds on each side. Drain on a paper towel. Place half a sheet of nori on the rolling mat and, leaving about 12 mm uncovered, spread prepared sushi rice over the rest of the sheet.

Spread one teaspoon of mayonnaise over the rice, followed by one teaspoon of unagi sauce. Cut one of the crabs in half and place on top of the rice along with a slice of avocado, a strip of cucumber and some watercress. Roll the nori until it completely covers the rice. Cut into four slices. Make three more rolls with the remaining ingredients.

ingredients

- Prepared sushi rice
- 2 sheets nori, cut in half lengthwise
- 4 fresh soft shell crabs
- Flour for coating
- 4 teaspoons tobiko (flying fish roe)
- Oil for frying
- 4 teaspoons mayonnaise
- 4 slices ripe avocado
- 4 strips cucumber
- Watercress
- Ready-made unagi sauce

spicy tuna roll

ingredients

- Prepared sushi rice
- 2 sheets nori
- 1 fresh tuna steak
- 1 cucumber
- 1 avocado (optional)
- 1 teaspoon smelt eggs
- 1/4 teaspoon mayonnaise
- 1/2 teaspoon hot sauce or chilli sauce
- Sesame seeds

method

Cut the tuna into thin strips. Mix the fish with the mayonnaise, smelt eggs and chilli sauce, adding the sesame seed oil and sesame seeds. If the taste is too spicy, add a little more mayonnaise. Put aside. Slice the cucumber and avocado into strips and assemble the roll on nori sheets using the rice as a base. Spread the spicy tuna mix and cucumber and add the avocado if desired. Roll and serve as usual.

alaska roll

Obviously if you make an Alaska roll, you should include something from Alaska – the Alaskan King Crab is the special ingredient needed to make this roll perfect. However, they don't grow on trees so if you can't find one, don't despair, any crab meat is fine.

method

Slice the salmon and cucumber into thin strips. Arrange all the ingredients over the rice. Once again, don't add wasabi to the centre of this roll, it will detract from the gentle flavours which are its secret strength.

ingredients

- Prepared sushi rice
- 2 sheets nori
- 30 g crab meat, flaked
- 30 g mild flavoured smoked salmon, cut into strips
- $\frac{1}{2}$ cucumber, cut into strips
- 3-4 tablespoons of cream cheese

uramaki (inside-out roll)

Once you have mastered the first two styles of roll, try a more impressive inside-out roll which will leave you beaming with pride.

spread and turn

Place a sheet of nori on the mat as before and spread prepared sushi rice evenly over the nori. Cover with plastic wrap and press evenly. Turn the ingredients over so that the nori is now on top and the plastic wrap is on the mat. Lay strips of fish or vegetables in the centre of the nori.

filling suggestions:

- Salmon and cucumber
- Crab, cucumber, and avocado
- Spicy tuna and red pepper
- Prawn tempura, green onion and eel sauce

roll and serve

With ingredients which are difficult to roll, a little rice laid in a strip along the centre can help to bind the other ingredients. Lift the edge of the bamboo mat along with the plastic wrap and fold it over. Treat the roll like a maki roll and compress the ingredients to ensure they stick together. When you unroll the mat, however, carefully remove the plastic wrap. At this point you could add some fish roe or sesame seeds along the top to add more style and flavour. Slice the roll into bite-sized portions and serve. Using the same methods described above, try your favourite fillings from the temaki and futomaki sections in a uramaki style. Adding a little wasabi to the centre of the roll gives extra zest, but be careful not to make the ingredients too wet or it will not roll successfully.

temaki sushi (hand-rolled)

One of the best ways to share a sushi experience with friends is to serve them temaki sushi, or hand-rolled sushi. All you do is prepare the ingredients in advance, arrange them on a tray in the middle of the table and start experimenting.

form the cone

To make hand-rolled sushi, spoon some sushi rice onto a diagonally cut sheet of nori. Place it towards the centre of the nori leaving space either side which will be the flap for sealing the roll. Keep most of the ingredients towards what will become the top of the roll. Form the cone shape with your hands, keeping the ingredients tight in the nori. Moisten the edge of the nori and seal.

vegetable fillings

Fresh vegetables such as thin strips of carrot, finely sliced green onion, red pepper, avocado and cucumber are ideal as accompaniments or on their own. Spicy mayonnaise and wasabi will enhance the roll.

meat and fish

Almost anything will go well with the taste of sushi rice and nori. Try rare roast beef, strips of cooked chicken, fish roe, smoked salmon, or any cooked fish. Prawn or vegetable tempura adds crunch and heat, which is a mouthwatering combination.

Temaki sushi is a fun way to enjoy sushi but you may want to serve nigiri and uramaki rolls as well; just for those guests that can't wait to get stuck in!

mushroom and salmon delight

method

Soak the dried mushrooms in warm water for thirty minutes. Drain the water, reserving 60 ml. Remove the stems and cut the caps into thin strips. Place in a pan with the reserved water, sugar, mirin, and two tablespoons of shoyu and cook for ten minutes. Allow to cool. Prepare the prawns by peeling, de-veining and lightly boiling. Drain and slice in half horizontally and allow to cool. Slice the tuna and smoked salmon into 12 mm thin pieces. Peel, stone and thinly slice the avocado.

Lightly grill both sides of the nori sheets and cut each one into four squares. Take one square of nori in your palm, add a little rice spreading it with a spatula or fork. Wrap the prepared ingredients.

ingredients

- Prepared sushi rice
- 8 sheets nori
- 225 g of fresh tuna
- 100 g of smoked salmon
- 8 raw king prawns
- 1 avocado
- 4-5 dried mushrooms
- $1/3$ cucumber, shredded
- 2 tablespoons of shoyu
- 1 tablespoon mirin

crab temaki

ingredients

- Prepared sushi rice
- 4 sheets nori
- Imitation crab stick
- Prawns
- Avocado
- Crispy lettuce
- 2–3 teaspoons mayonnaise
- 1 teaspoon shoyu

method

Mix the mayonnaise and shoyu and put aside. Slice the avocado and lettuce into narrow strips. Quickly brown one sheet of nori until it is slightly crisp. Do not overheat or the nori will shrivel. Cut each sheet in half.

For each temaki, spread one teaspoon of the mayonnaise mixture diagonally from upper corner to centre of lower edge of nori. Place three tablespoons of rice along the same line. Lay a piece of crab stick, a slice of avocado, and a piece of lettuce leaf over the rice. Roll the nori into a cone shape, like an ice cream cone and top with a couple of small prawns. Repeat using the remaining ingredients. If sushi is not to be served immediately, cover with a damp tea towel. Never refrigerate sushi, and eat as soon as possible. Serve with pickled ginger and a shoyu dip.

temaki party special

Adjust the quantities of this recipe to make mouthwatering treats for any party.

method

Slice the aubergine into thin strips and quickly grill. Slice the tofu and then crisp by quickly frying at a good heat. Slice all the other vegetables into thin strips. Briefly grill each nori sheet, taking care not to burn them. Place a half sheet of nori horizontally in front of you on your mat. Place the rice on the left-hand third of nori, leaving a clear border of nori all around. Place a selection of the filling vertically across the middle of the rice. Fold the near corner of the nori over to begin folding into a cone shape. Continue to roll until a cone is formed. Adjust the combination of fillings with each new temaki.

ingredients

- Prepared sushi rice
- Sheets of nori
- Avocado
- Carrot
- Aubergine
- Tofu
- Tomato
- Cucumber
- Asparagus
- Spinach
- Green and yellow peppers
- Green onions

glossary

Aburaage	fried tofu pouches prepared by cooking in sweet cooking sake
Aemono	vegetables or meats mixed with a dressing or sauce
Agari	a Japanese sushi bar term for green tea
Agemono	fried foods, either deep-fat fried or pan-fried
Aji-no-moto	monosodium glutamate (msg)
Ama ebi	raw prawns
Anago	conger eel
Awabi	abalone
Azuki	small red beans
Beni shoga	red pickled ginger
Biiru	beer
Buri toro	fatty belly strip of the yellowtail
Buta	pork
Chikuwa	browned fish cake with a hole running through its length
Chirashi sushi	scattered sushi
Chutoro	marbled tuna belly
Daikon	white radish
Dashi	basic Japanese stock
Donburi	a large bowl for noodle and rice dishes
Ebi	cooked prawns
Fugu	puffer fish
Fukusa sushi	a type of sushi which is wrapped in a crêpe

Futomaki	large sushi roll
Gari	pickled ginger
Gobou	burdock root
Gohan	plain boiled rice
Goma	sesame seeds
Gunkan maki	battleship sushi
Ha	leaves
Hagiri	rice-cooling tub
Hamachi	young yellowtail
Hamaguri	clam
Hashi	chopsticks
Hirame	flat fish with eyes on the left such as brill or turbot
Hocho	general term for knives
Hokagai	surf clam
Hotate-gai	scallop
Ika	squid
Ikura	salmon roe
Inari	fried pouches of tofu stuffed with sushi rice
Kaki	oyster
Kampyo	dried gourd
Kani	crab
Katsuo-bushi	bonito shavings
Kazunoko	herring roe
Kombo	kelp
Kuro goma	black sesame seeds
Maguro	tuna fish

Makisu	mat made of bamboo strips for making sushi rolls	**Shamoji**	flat rice-serving spoon/spatula
Manaita	chopping board	**Sashimi**	raw fish served sliced
Masu	trout	**Shime sabe**	marinated mackerel
Mirin	sweet rice wine for cooking	**Shiro goma**	white sesame seeds
Mirugai	surf clam	**Shiro miso**	white soya bean paste
Miso	soya bean paste	**Shiitake**	Japanese mushroom
Moyashi	bean sprouts	**Shouga**	ginger root
Natto	fermented soya beans	**Shoyu**	Japanese soy sauce
Negi	spring onion	**Su**	rice vinegar
Neta	the piece of fish that is placed on top of the sushi rice for nigiri	**Suzuki**	sea bass
		Tai	sea bream
Nigiri sushi	fingers of rice topped with wasabi and raw or cooked fish and shellfish	**Takenoko**	bamboo shoots
		Tako	octopus
		Tamago	egg
Nori	sheets of dried seaweed	**Temaki sushi**	hand-rolled sushi
Ocha	tea	**Tempura**	seafood or vegetables dipped in a light batter and deep fried
Ohyo garei	halibut		
Oshibori	the wet towel one cleans one's hands with before the meal	**Tobiko**	flying fish roe
		Tofu	soya bean curd
Oshi-sushi	sushi made from rice pressed in a box or mould	**Toriniku**	chicken
		Uchiwa	fan
Oshi waku	wooden box with top	**Unagi**	freshwater eel
Renkon	lotus root	**Uni**	sea urchin
Saba	mackerel	**Uramaki**	inside-out sushi roll
Sake	salmon	**Usukuchi shoyu**	light Japanese soy sauce
Sansho	Japanese pepper	**Wasabi**	Japanese horseradish
Sashimi-bouchou	sushi knife		

useful phrases

Domo arigato – Thank you

Douzo – Please

Gaijin – Outsiders, foreigners

Gochisoo sama deshita – Thanks for the meal

Hebereke – Drunk

Itadakimasu – Traditional phrase opening a meal

Kampai – Cheers

Konnichiwa – Hello/good afternoon

Nemui – Sleepy

Onakagasuita – Hungry

Sakana – Fish

Shinsen – Fresh

Tanoshii – Enjoyable, fun